Daily Life in SHANG DYNASTY CHINA

Lori Hile

heinemann raintree

Edited by Linda Staniford and Holly Beaumont
Designed by Philippa Jenkins
Original illustrations © Capstone Global Library Limited 2015
Illustrated by Oxford Designers and Illustrators; caption character and pages 42–43 by Philippa Jenkins
Picture research by Gina Kammer
Production by Victoria Fitzgerald
Originated by Capstone Global Library Ltd

Library of Congress Cataloging-in-Publication Data
Cataloging-in-publication data is available at the Library of Congress.
ISBN 978-1-4846-2579-8 (paperback)
ISBN 978-1-4846-2592-7 (ebook PDF)

This book has been officially leveled by using the F&P Text Level Gradient™ Leveling System.

Acknowledgments
The author and publisher are grateful to the following for permission to reproduce copyright material: Alamy: © China Images, 13, © China Images, 14, 38, © TAO Images Limited, 37, © World History Archive, 15; Art Resource, N.Y.: © BnF, Dist. RMN-Grand Palais, 5; Bridgeman Images: Gift of Charles Lang Freer/Freer Gallery of Art, Smithsonian Institution, USA/Bracelet (jade), Chinese School, Shang Dynasty (1766-1050 bce), 24; Corbis: © Asian Art & Archaeology, Inc., 9, (bottom) 21, 27, © Imaginechina, 16, © Keren Su, 22, © Lowell Georgia, 12; Getty Images: Blend Images - Jade, 35, DEA PICTURE LIBRARY, 25, James Burke, 30, 36, Science & Society Picture Library, 22; Glow Images: Superstock, 10; Granger, NYC: 6, 11; Science Source, 7; Shutterstock: Andrey_Popov, 33, Hung Chung Chih, 41, Jack.Q, 19, Monika Wisniewska, 32, noppharat, (top) 21, 26, Peter Stuckings, 29, sunxuejun, 40, Suppakij1017, 23; Smithsonian Institution, Washington D.C.: Freer Gallery of Art/Purchase, F1936.6a-b, cover; Wikimedia, 8.

Cover image: A bronze ritual vessel in the shape of an elephant. This would have been used to offer sacrifices of food or wine to the Shang gods.

We would like to thank Dr. Yijie Zhuang for his help in the preparation of this book.

Printed in the United States of America.
010535RP

CONTENTS

Some words are shown in bold, **like this.** You can find out what they mean by looking in the glossary.

In northern China, the modern city of Anyang is sandwiched between one of the world's largest rivers and a group of towering mountains. Over 3,500 years ago, this land was dotted with marketplaces selling gorgeous silk clothes and shiny bronze dishes, farms with crops and animals, and grand palaces protected by thick, tall walls. Behind those walls lived the ruling **emperors**. But these men ruled differently from most leaders today.

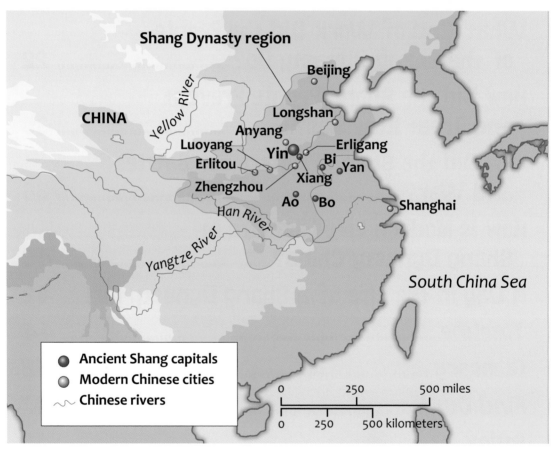

Shang Dynasty region

Beijing

Yellow River

CHINA

Longshan

Anyang

Luoyang

Erlitou

Yin

Erligang

Bi

Yan

Zhengzhou

Xiang

Han River

Ao

Bo

Shanghai

Yangtze River

South China Sea

- ● **Ancient Shang capitals**
- ● **Modern Chinese cities**
- ∿ **Chinese rivers**

| 0 | 250 | 500 miles |

| 0 | 250 | 500 kilometers |

The Shang dynasty was located in the northeastern region of what is now modern China.

The end of the Xia

Before the Shang dynasty, the Xia ruled the region. Early Chinese historians say that the last Xia king was a dishonest tyrant and his people were unhappy. For many years, another tribe fought to overthrow the unpopular king. Usually the king and his family fought wars, but a tribal leader named Cheng Tang gave weapons to the **peasants**. Together, they defeated the Xia in the Battle of Mingtiao and established the Shang dynasty.

Welcome to Shang dynasty China

Many countries today choose their rulers by voting. But in ancient China, large groups of relatives called clans or tribes fought with other tribes for power. The family that won got to rule the region. When a ruler died, the family passed the power on to another family member. This family would rule until they were overthrown by another tribe.

This system of governing is called a dynasty. The first dynasty we have records for is the Shang, which began around 1600 BCE. The Shang dynasty occupied a large area in northern China, on both sides of the Yellow River. It was led by over 30 different emperors, operating out of several different capital cities, and lasted over 600 years, until about 1040 BCE.

How did the emperor affect daily life?

Since Chinese emperors won their power through battles or birthright rather than elections, they had to convince their subjects they had a right to rule. They did this by claiming that it was the will of the gods. An emperor would have to prove he was supposed to be in charge by governing well and wisely—if things went wrong, it might mean he was not pleasing the gods and should no longer be in charge.

The first emperor, Cheng Tang

In a book called *The Biographies of Emperors*, the founder of the Shang dynasty, Cheng Tang, is described as "9 feet [2.7 meters] in height, with the **virtue** of a saint." This description must be exaggerated, but most historians agree that Cheng Tang was an honest and fair ruler who genuinely cared about both people and animals.

The Yellow Emperor

The Chinese have long told stories about an emperor named Huang Di, who lived 1,000 years before the Shang dynasty. He is said to have invented writing, medicine, the first calendar, the pottery wheel, and the magnetic compass. However, these inventions probably took place over thousands of years. Huang Di was nicknamed "The Yellow Emperor," because emperors were thought to be molded from yellow earth. For thousands of years in China, only emperors could wear yellow clothing or have a yellow roof, in honor of Huang Di.

However, if the ruler was cruel or dishonest, or if natural disasters such as floods, droughts, or earthquakes happened during his reign, the people would question his right to rule. Another tribe might also overthrow him.

The Shang calendar was built around a year of 360 days, split equally among 12 months.

Boy power

If you grew up in the Shang dynasty's ruling tribe, you had a chance to be emperor one day...that's if you were a boy. Chinese dynasties were dominated by men. Fathers ruled households, and emperors ruled the government. When an emperor died, the crown was passed on to his oldest son. If the emperor didn't have a son, his younger brother would rule.

Powerful women

Women in the Shang ruling family couldn't govern, but they could become powerful. Around 1200 BCE, Fu ("Lady" in Chinese) Hao, a wife of King Wu Ding, became a successful military leader (see page 38 to discover more about her). Because of this, some historians believe that women in the Shang dynasty enjoyed more power than women at other times in Chinese history.

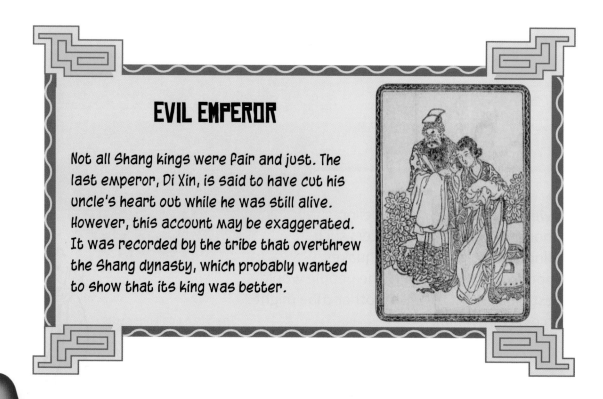

EVIL EMPEROR

Not all Shang kings were fair and just. The last emperor, Di Xin, is said to have cut his uncle's heart out while he was still alive. However, this account may be exaggerated. It was recorded by the tribe that overthrew the Shang dynasty, which probably wanted to show that its king was better.

Hunting parties and other courtly duties

Ruling the kingdom required constant attention. Tribes living outside the city often threatened to invade Shang territory, so the emperor frequently visited tribal leaders to keep up friendly relations and remind them of his power. If the tribes attacked, the emperor defended Shang territory.

During peaceful periods, the emperor often went on long hunting trips. There, he and his advisers would kill tigers, elephants, rhinoceroses, and other animals for food, clothing, and religious **sacrifices**. The emperor also attended the births and funerals of nobles and participated in religious rituals.

On royal hunts, the emperor and the other nobles used weapons like this bronze axe. They practiced skills they needed in battle.

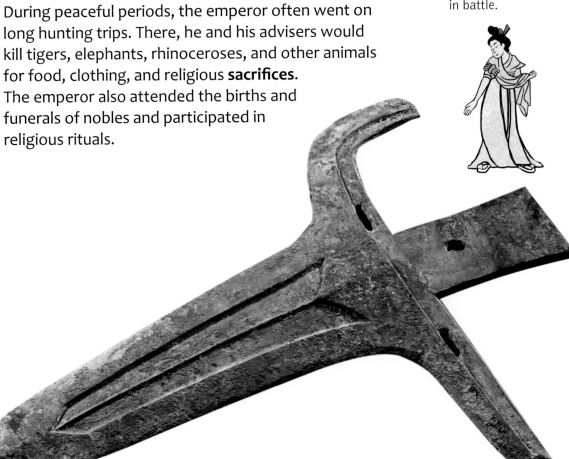

The Shang believed in many gods, but one towered over the rest: Shangdi. Just as the emperor ruled over humans on Earth, Shangdi ruled over gods and nature from heaven. This supreme god was so powerful that humans couldn't communicate with him directly. Instead, the emperor had to send messages, questions, or prayers to the spirits of his dead relatives, who would pass them along to Shangdi.

The emperor also prayed to spirits of the natural world. The Shang believed that the wind god sent lightning and thunder, while the river gods could bring rain.

The Shang believed the spirits of their ancestors could travel between heaven and "Below Heaven," where humans lived.

FRIENDLY DRAGONS

In many Western fairy tales, dragons are fearsome creatures. With huge, lizard-like bodies, horns, and bat-like wings, they breathed fire and scared humans. But in Chinese legend, dragons are symbols of good luck. These cute, snake-like creatures were said to live in the water and affect the weather. When the mischievous dragons raced down a river they caused floods, and when they played in the clouds they caused rain. During dangerous droughts, the Chinese people offered them sacrifices. They also tried to bring rain by burning clay dragons.

Sacrifices to the gods

The Shang tried to please their gods with elaborate sacrifices. Nobles served them food and wine in fancy bronze ritual vessels and offered them freshly killed animals. Some vessels were decorated with pictures of the animals sacrificed.

Humans were also offered to the gods. In fact, some experts believe that at least 13,000 humans were sacrificed during the Shang dynasty. These people were usually slaves who were sacrificed at religious rituals, important funerals, and the construction of new buildings. If slaves protested against their sacrifice, the Shang emperor sometimes threatened to kill their children.

Talking to the dead

To rule effectively, the emperor needed information from his ancestors about what the future held. To find answers, a scribe carved the emperor's question onto a turtle shell or a bone from an ox or deer. Then the scribe drilled holes into the underside of the shell and applied heat. Soon, cracks would appear. A type of fortune-teller called a **diviner** would read the cracks as messages from the emperor's dead relatives during a ceremony known as a divination.

For example, the scribe might write the question, "Will there be any disasters within the next 10 days?" By looking at the pattern in the cracks, the diviner would determine if the answer was "yes," "no," or "undecided."

WERE DIVINERS EVER WRONG?

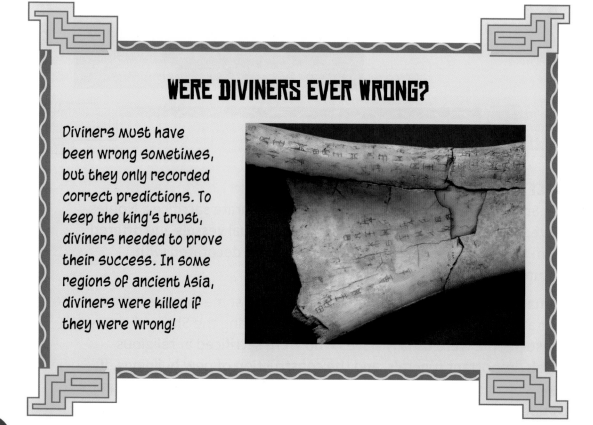

Diviners must have been wrong sometimes, but they only recorded correct predictions. To keep the king's trust, diviners needed to prove their success. In some regions of ancient Asia, diviners were killed if they were wrong!

Hundreds of oracle bones have been discovered near modern-day Anyang.

Importance of oracle bones

These inscribed shells and bones were called oracle bones, and they provide many important clues about daily life in Shang dynasty China. From the inscriptions, we know that Shang emperors wondered about battle outcomes, sacrifices, illnesses, and the weather. We also learn the names of many Shang rulers, and the oracle bones provide us with the earliest examples of Chinese writing, which was well developed by 1500 BCE.

HOW DO WE KNOW?

Oracle bones and shells were first sold in the late 19th century as "dragon's bones," an ingredient in traditional Chinese medicine. When writing was discovered on the bones, **archaeologists** searched the site where the bones were found, near Anyang. So far, archaeologists have recovered fragments of at least 150,000 oracle bones.

Secrets of the tombs

The Shang believed that dead people changed form but continued to live the same kind of life. So, dead musicians needed instruments, dead rich people needed money and jewels, and dead warriors needed weapons. These items were often buried with the dead in tombs.

Much of what we know about the Shang comes from these objects. The rich had grand tombs filled with bronze vases, pottery, food, oracle bones, clothes, jewelry, and weapons. Jade objects were also common. This hard, green, white, or purple stone was believed to have magical powers to chase away evil spirits. We know less about peasants, since they often had no tombs or objects buried with them.

One of the best-preserved Shang tombs ever found was that of Lady Hao.

Accompanying in death

Shang nobles were buried with carriages for transportation and with servants. The idea was that faithful attendants should continue serving their masters in the next life. These people were probably a combination of the king's real servants, guards, workers, and slaves. In one tomb alone, over 500 human skeletons were found. In some graves, the king's attendants were even buried with their own attendants.

The idea of "accompanying in death" was practiced in several ancient cultures. In ancient Egypt, the pharaoh (king) sometimes had servants buried with him. By 225 BCE, the Chinese replaced human victims with **wicker** figurines or life-size statues made of wood or terra-cotta.

MAN'S BEST FRIEND

In ancient Egypt, cats were adored and even **mummified**. In Shang dynasty China, dogs enjoyed a special place in society. Dogs were used in hunts and probably kept as pets. In one large Shang tomb, archaeologists unearthed the skeleton of a dog buried in its own grave.

Shang cities had strong walls separating them into two parts. The inner walls housed the emperor's palace and the ancestral temple, where religious rituals and divinations took place. Inside these walls, you would also find a treasury and military **barracks**. Outside the walls were workshops, burial places, trading centers, and homes for ordinary people. Walkways connected the two parts of the city, and narrow ditches underneath major buildings drained waste and rainwater away.

Homes

Wealthy people or nobles probably lived in palaces. These looked like large rectangles perched on top of raised earth platforms. They did not use stone for walls or tiles for roofs. Instead, roofs were covered with dried vegetation (such as straw or reeds) and supported by pillars or walls made of sand, soil, and clay.

Ordinary people were not so lucky. Their homes were small, round huts, buried partially underground. The walls were made of a mixture of sand, soil, and clay called stamped earth, with straw roofs. Large families lived together in one or two rooms.

Shang emperors lived in palaces like this one, which was re-created near the ancient Shang capital of Yin, near modern-day Anyang.

DO NOT ENTER

The walls surrounding the ancient Shang capital of Zhengzhou were about 4.3 miles (7 kilometers) long, 60 feet (18 meters) wide, and as high as a three-story building. It probably took 10,000 workers at least 18 years to build these strong walls.

Shang cities housed palaces, temples, marketplaces, and workshops.

Family Life

Families were extremely important to the ancient Chinese. A family home would include mother, father, and children, but also grandparents, aunts, uncles, and cousins. Children were taught to treat their elders with great respect. Even after their relatives died, the Chinese honored them with prayers and sacrifices at altars in their homes. They believed their relatives continued to watch over the family as spirits.

Men ruled Shang households, and boys were valued more than girls. Most Chinese families prayed for boys, and some even left baby girls outside to die. When Fu Hao gave birth to a girl, oracle bones described it as "unfortunate."

Stay-at-home school

Instead of going to school, it's likely that Shang children learned from their parents and grandparents. Wealthy boys and girls learned reading, writing, and arithmetic. Peasant children learned more practical skills like farming or craftmaking. As teenagers, they began to work in the fields or family store.

This symbol means "learning" in the picture-writing of China.

Language

To read, we just need to memorize 26 letters and use them in different combinations. The ancient Chinese, however, had to memorize different symbols, called characters, for every word. The same basic writing system is still used today, making Chinese the oldest written language in the world.

Newspapers printed in Chinese can be read and understood by people all across China.

Even in modern times, Chinese people from different regions speak different languages. But people from these different regions can communicate in writing.

A LANGUAGE OF SOUND

The Chinese have several spoken languages, but only one written language. Since each character stands for an idea, not a sound, different regions created different sounds for the same symbols. In the same way, both French and English people use the same numerical symbols, such as "2" or "3," but pronounce them completely differently.

What's for dinner?

Wealthy people would eat meat from animals captured during royal hunts. This might include rhinoceroses, tigers, birds, and other **game**. They would also feast on animals killed for sacrifices, such as oxen, pigs, and chickens. And they might enjoy turtle meat, stripped from the shells that were used for oracle bones.

Poor people would probably eat cereal or stew made from millet (a type of grain) for breakfast, lunch, and dinner, along with the occasional plate of noodles or soybeans. Everyone would have eaten fish caught in the river and probably snacked on chestnuts, mulberries, apricots, and berries.

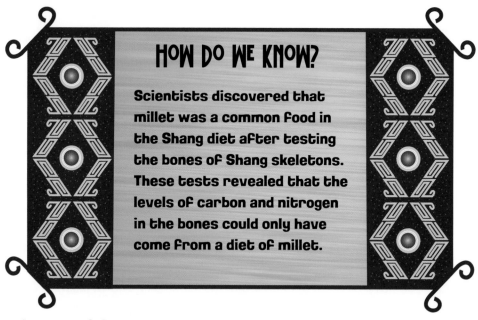

HOW DO WE KNOW?

Scientists discovered that millet was a common food in the Shang diet after testing the bones of Shang skeletons. These tests revealed that the levels of carbon and nitrogen in the bones could only have come from a diet of millet.

Clothing and jewelry

Shang peasants probably dressed in simple **hemp** garments. The rich would have worn silk and adorned themselves with bracelets, necklaces, earrings, belts, and hairpins made of jade and precious stones. Winter nights in the region are cold, so it's likely that the Shang people wrapped themselves in animal skins, like many ancient people.

SECRET SILK

Perhaps even as far back as 3000 BCE, the Chinese became the first culture to discover that tiny caterpillars, known as silkworms, could produce shimmering silk. The Chinese silk-making process was a closely guarded secret. Anyone who removed silkworm eggs or cocoons from China or revealed silk-making secrets to a foreigner was put to death. Silk was so valuable that it was sometimes used as money. Only the upper **class** could afford to wear it.

∧ Silkworm caterpillars spin cocoons with a single strand of silk thread, up to 3,000 feet (900 meters) long!

Shang dynasty nobles wore jade jewelry as a way to show their high status in society.

What will you be when you grow up? If you were born in Shang dynasty China, your answer would probably depend on who your parents were. Shang citizens usually stayed in the same social class their entire lives and learned their trade from family members.

The highest-ranking class was the nobility. Royal officials supervised the royal stables and palaces, craftworkers' workshops, building projects, and territories outside the city. They also led armies during wars. Royal diviners, **astronomers**, and **astrologers** helped the emperor to make important decisions.

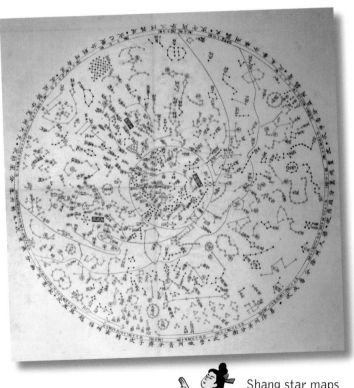

Shang star maps included over 40 constellations and 140 stars.

ASTONISHING ACCURACY

As early as 1500 BCE, the Chinese believed that it took 365.25 days for Earth to circle the Sun, which is extremely close to the actual time of 365.24219.

FRIGHTENED BY DRAGONS

Imagine it's a sunny summer day when suddenly the sky turns as dark as night. This rare natural event, called a total solar eclipse, happens when the Moon completely blocks the Sun's light from Earth. The event frightened the ancient Chinese, who believed that a dragon was eating the Sun. They would scream and bang on pots and drums to try to frighten away the dragon. Sometimes they also blamed the emperor, believing he had angered the gods. To keep his people free from fear, it was important that the king predict these events and reassure his people they were part of a heavenly plan.

Looking to the skies

Ancient Greek astronomers studied the sky because they wondered how the universe worked. But the Chinese were more practical. They studied the sky to help the emperor plan events and warn his subjects about natural disasters.

Shang astronomers made complex maps of the stars and understood that the position of the stars signaled the changing seasons. Knowing when the **monsoon** season or spring thaw would occur helped the emperor to decide when his farmers should plant their crops or prepare for floods.

Artisans and craftworkers

Unlike most ordinary people, artisans and craftworkers lived in above-ground houses with stamped-earth floors. They worked in government workshops and were valued for their special skills at creating magnificent objects.

Artisans created precious metal and stone earrings, necklaces, belt buckles, and hairpins for the wealthy. They carved intricate jade jewelry. This shiny green stone was so hard that only an even harder stone, like diamond, could carve it. It probably took artisans a year to carve even a small jade piece.

During the Shang dynasty, more people started wearing jewelry made from jade.

Shang vessels are considered some of the world's greatest art objects.

The Bronze Age

The thing that truly set Shang artisans apart from earlier artists was their skill with bronze. Around 2000 BCE, the Chinese learned that mixing the soft metals copper and tin together made a sturdier golden substance called bronze. This was the beginning of China's Bronze Age, which lasted until about 400 BCE.

Bronze plows and tools would have helped farmers, but the emperor ordered bronze factories to produce weapons and chariot fittings. Since metal was expensive, only the nobles could afford to use these weapons in war. They fought with sharp spearheads, arrowheads, knives, and axes, while peasants used inferior stone weapons. This discouraged the peasants from attempting to overthrow the nobles.

Artisans also created fancy bronze pots and drinking vessels for religious ceremonies. These were decorated with images of real and imaginary animals, such as birds, tigers, elephants, and dragons. Some of the containers were also shaped like animals, with the wine poured out of the beak or mouth.

Farming the land

Farmers were highly respected in Shang dynasty China. Without food, the entire society would have collapsed. Since farming was such an important industry, the Shang emperor served as a leader and adviser to farmers. He performed the ritual first planting of the season and asked the gods for guidance about when and what to plant. Inscriptions on oracle bones included questions like: "Should the king lead the many people in planting grain?" and "When we reach the fourth month, will Di (the high god) make it rain?"

Millet, like most of the crops in the Shang dynasty, was irrigated using water from the Yellow River.

Oxen, like the one in this stone carving, were used by the ancient Chinese to pull plows.

Fruits of their Labor

By the time of the Shang dynasty, farmers raised animals such as cows, oxen, water buffalo, ducks, and chicken for food, labor, and ritual sacrifices. They also grew drought-resistant crops, such as wheat, millet, and hemp seed.

Another change during the Shang dynasty was the widespread farming of the soybean. Around 1100 BCE, the Shang learned that soybeans grew well in all conditions and enriched the soil with nutrients. They also discovered soybeans were high in protein. Soon, soybeans became a staple (main food) in the Chinese diet and were used to make tofu, soy sauce, miso, and soy milk. Rice, the grain commonly associated with China, was mostly grown in southern regions of the country.

ANIMALS AT WORK

The Shang were among the first ancient people to put animals to work. Water buffaloes pulled heavy plows, and horses drew carts and carriages. European countries didn't put animals to work for another 1,000 years.

To market, to market

In Shang society, merchants ranked under almost everyone except slaves. Unlike artisans and farmers, merchants didn't produce any useful products themselves. Instead, they bought and sold things others made—sometimes for twice their original price. This was considered dishonorable. But merchants could gain wealth and power. Some of them built huge palaces, and some of their daughters married nobles. In an early historical document, one writer complained that "Merchants neither plow nor weed, but they ride in well-built cars and whip up fat horses, wear shoes of silk, and trail white silk behind them."

Slaves

Slaves, however, had no wealth or power. They performed the same types of jobs as other common people, such as building tombs, farming, and bronze-making, but they could also be used as human sacrifices. These unfortunate individuals included those who could not pay their debts, criminals, prisoners captured in war, and the children of slaves.

It was mostly slaves who built Shang's magnificent tombs and strong walls, which could take 30 to 40 years to complete. This meant a slave might toil his entire life on a single project, only to be sacrificed to the gods when finished. Fortunately, owners sometimes freed loyal slaves after years of faithful service, and the government occasionally set slaves free.

Even though they were not valued highly by the rich, the common people of Shang dynasty China were the ones who created the clothing, tombs, jewelry, vessels, and weapons that made the region so vibrant.

Slaves toiled over Shang structures for many years with little reward. Even as thousands-year-old ruins from an ancient Chinese capital, these walls still stand strong!

When we get sick, we blame an infection. The Shang believed that people got sick after upsetting an ancestor or after an evil spirit entered their bodies. In order to be cured, patients needed to please their ancestors or get rid of the demon. A type of healer called a shaman would sometimes consult oracle bones to find out which ancestors were angry and how to make them happy. Shamans also drove away the evil spirits through "exorcisms," a ritual in which they ordered the spirit to leave the body.

Chinese ritual masks were used during exorcism ceremonies to drive out the evil spirits causing illness.

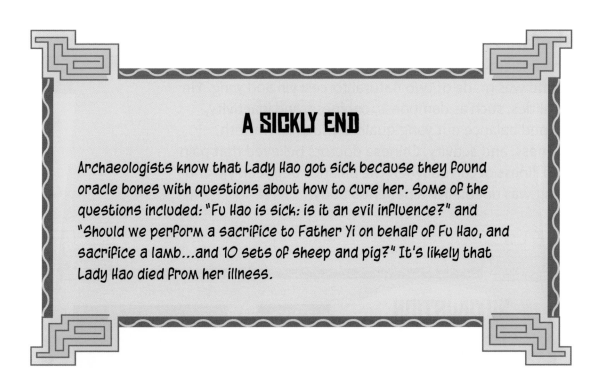

A SICKLY END

Archaeologists know that Lady Hao got sick because they found oracle bones with questions about how to cure her. Some of the questions included: "Fu Hao is sick: is it an evil influence?" and "Should we perform a sacrifice to Father Yi on behalf of Fu Hao, and sacrifice a lamb...and 10 sets of sheep and pig?" It's likely that Lady Hao died from her illness.

Six evils

The ancient Chinese believed that six evil spirits could invade people's bodies to make them sick. The Chinese lived close to nature and saw these spirits as natural energies: wind, cold, dampness, heat, summer heat, and dryness. Just as these energies affected the environment, they affected a person's body. For instance, joint pain from arthritis was seen as a "cold" illness, since cold weather increased the pain, while heat could reduce it.

Keeping well

Traditional Shang doctors tried to treat people before they got sick. They believed that treating a sick person was like making weapons after starting a battle. By then, it might be too late!

Health: A balancing act

The ancient Chinese believed that everything in the world was made of two natural forces: *yin* and *yang*. Yin qualities, such as dampness, coolness, and inactivity, helped balance out yang qualities, such as warmth, dryness, and activity. Chinese doctors believed that pain and illness occurred when the balance between yin and yang was unequal in a patient's body.

MOXIBUSTION

Shang doctors sometimes used a treatment called moxibustion. Small cones, dried leaves, and certain types of plants were burned above special places on the patient's body. The ashes were rubbed into the body where blisters formed. This method is still used today in many parts of Asia.

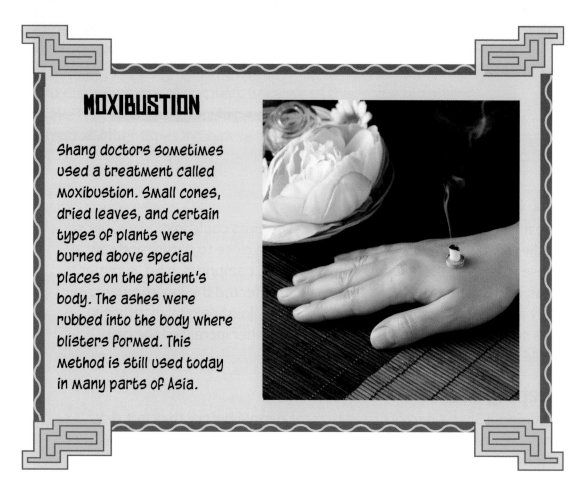

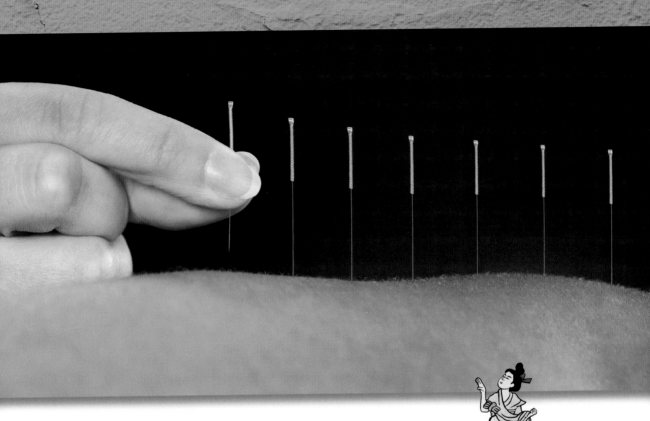

Back in balance

To help restore the balance, traditional Chinese doctors would advise their patients to eat certain foods, drink certain teas, or perform certain exercises. The doctor might also provide herbal medicines.

Acupuncture

Of course, a doctor might also decide to stick you with needles! The ancient Chinese believed that a form of energy called *qi* flowed through our bodies. When we are healthy, this energy flows freely, like water flowing through a hose. But when we are sick or in pain, this flow of energy is blocked. Doctors tried to restore the flow of *qi* by placing thin, sharp needles into points along a patient's body. Early in the Shang dynasty, stone needles were used but later needles were made of bone.

This method of treatment, called **acupuncture**, is still used today to treat everything from arthritis and asthma to headaches and eye diseases.

Acupuncture needles are not always placed at the point of illness. For example, placing needles at certain points on the foot might help the liver.

The secret to everlasting life?

Do you want to live forever? If so, you're not alone! In many ancient cultures, including China, a group of people called **alchemists** tried combining different substances in the hopes of discovering the elixir of life. They believed that this special combination of ingredients would restore youth, cure diseases, improve mental and physical powers, and make humans immortal.

Alchemists began by searching for ways to change common metals into gold. Since gold lasts forever, they thought the same process could extend human life. They learned that mixing two soft metals, copper and tin, produced a harder metal called bronze. Alchemists also mixed metals with chemicals like mercury and arsenic and believed that swallowing a pea-sized quantity of this combination would make humans *"hsien,"* or immortal. But mercury and arsenic are deadly poisons—and several emperors probably died from swallowing them.

Alchemists never achieved their goals, but their observations about chemical reactions became the basis for modern chemistry. And their experiments with plants and minerals helped them discover healing drugs that are still used today.

HOW DO WE KNOW?

Chinese legend says that "The Yellow Emperor" wrote the first major Chinese medical text around 2000 BCE. Most experts believe the book was actually written later, around 300 BCE. But many of the treatments described in the book, including acupuncture, were probably in their early stages during the Shang dynasty.

Jobs for girls

Medicine was one of the few professions open to women. Female midwives helped farm women deliver babies. Female doctors often treated ladies of the imperial court.

Chinese pharmacies today still create medicine using herbs and plants.

War was a way of life in Shang society. Tribes from outside territories often attacked without warning. The city walls helped protect citizens, and so did the mountains, but more protection was needed.

The king called on his ancestors, and he housed an army of about a thousand men at his capital. He proved his bravery by personally leading them into battle. If the king didn't fight, his subjects lost respect for him and sometimes tried to overthrow him. Other members of the nobility served alongside the king, and peasants and slaves were required to serve in the military whenever called upon.

The Shang army captured as many as 30,000 prisoners of war at a time. Nobles wore bronze helmets like this one.

HOW DO WE KNOW?

Oracle bones discovered near Anyang contained symbols of wheeled vehicles. Later, bronze fittings for chariots were found in royal tombs there. Then, in 1936, archaeologists found a huge burial pit containing two ancient chariots, along with the skeletons of four horses and three humans!

Oracle bones describe the Shang armies winning battles with chariots like this one.

Calling in the troops

Rulers of the neighboring city-states were also required to provide the king with military support. This helped the Shang king raise a large army—as many as 13,000 men in some wars.

Peasants and slaves trudged onto the battlefield on foot, while nobles entered in fine horse-drawn chariots. Each chariot transported a driver, an archer, and a soldier carrying a lance, a long, spear-like weapon.

CHINA'S FIRST RECORDED TRAFFIC ACCIDENT

Around 1250 BCE, Emperor Wu Ding was hunting rhinoceroses with his son, Prince Yang, when their chariot overturned. Prince Yang was probably badly hurt, because later oracle bones discussed rituals that would help him recover.

Lady Hao, woman warrior

Few women were allowed to hold jobs in ancient China. Fewer still became military commanders. But Lady Hao was different. Fu Hao was married to Shang emperor Wu Ding, who had 59 other wives-one from every neighboring tribe. But Lady Hao set herself apart with her intelligence, fearlessness, and beauty. The emperor trusted her to lead dozens of military campaigns, including one against the Tu-Fang tribe. The tribe had fought the Shang for decades, until they were finally defeated by Fu Hao in a single battle! Fu Hao also defeated the nearby Yi and Qiang tribes. She commanded over 13,000 soldiers and several important generals, making her the most powerful military leader of the time.

Bronze weapons

The ancient Chinese didn't have modern-day weapons, like guns and bombs. However, they had one big advantage over their neighboring tribes: bronze. While their neighbors used primitive wood and stone weapons, the Shang wielded strong dagger-axes, daggers, spears, and short swords glinting of this fine metal. Just knowing that the Shang had stronger weapons was sometimes enough to prevent other tribes from attacking.

Preparing for battle

To prepare for battle, the Shang practiced early forms of **martial arts**. Shang soldiers learned skills like chopping, stabbing, leaping, kicking, and tumbling to defend themselves against the enemy. Hunting was also good preparation for war. The ancient Chinese used a type of short stick called a cudgel to fight wild beasts, which also helped them on the battlefield. Also, the meat they hunted provided meals during wars.

THE BATTLE OF MUYE: THE END OF AN ERA

Shang ruler Di Xin was cruel and unpopular. During his reign, a tribe called the Zhou began gaining power. To stop them, Di Xin imprisoned their leader. This angered the leader's son, King Wu, who led an army into Shang territory. Di Xin ordered Shang soldiers to defend the capital and provided slaves with weapons, ordering them to fight. But the slaves and many soldiers turned their spears upside down. They didn't want to defend their cruel emperor. This battle led to the end of the Shang dynasty and the start of the Zhou dynasty.

If you visit China today, you'll find traces of the Shang dynasty wherever you look. Newspapers are printed with characters similar to the ones the Shang developed thousands of years ago. This writing system allowed people from different regions of China to read and write the same language.

The Shang idea of a walled city was used nearly 2,500 years later when the Forbidden City palace complex was built in Beijing.

Doctors still use traditional herbs, medicines, and acupuncture, just like Shang healers. In recent decades, Western nations have also adopted many of these practices. There are also still silk factories for transforming cocoons into beautiful silk garments.

Many children still live with their grandparents and show deep respect for their elders. Even though religious practice is not always encouraged by the current Chinese government, ancestor worship lasted in China for thousands of years. Until the early 1900s, dynasties still claimed that their right to rule China was the will of the gods. And, unfortunately, boys are still valued more than girls in China.

China still produces most of the world's silk.

Each new dynasty made changes but didn't change China's basic culture. Instead, they fought to preserve and build on the culture started by the Shang.

A Day in the Life of a Shang Dynasty Girl

My name is Zhi. I'm 10 years old. I wake up when I hear my mother clanking dishes at the end of our small hut. I also hear something I haven't heard lately: rain beating against our straw roof! Our family has been praying for rain to help my father's crops grow. He and my teenage brother are already in the fields. They spend their days planting millet, weeding vegetables, and feeding cows and chickens.

It's a cool spring morning, so I snuggle with my little sister on our low bed. When my grandmother calls my name, I finally rise.

My mother is heating water in a pot called a *li*. I help her stir in millet until the mixture is rich and creamy. My grandmother, mother, little sister, and I sit and eat our porridge from clay bowls.

After breakfast, I slip into a brown hemp tunic and weave my long, dark hair into a braid. My mother and I are going shopping. At the marketplace, I slide my hands over the smooth silk shoes, even though I know our family can only afford straw sandals. At the fish seller's tent, we trade a bag of millet for two carp. At the vegetable stand, we use cowrie shells to buy bok choy.

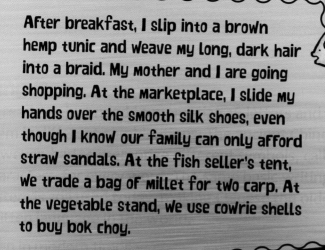

When my father returns home, he sits at the head of the table for our fish dinner. Afterward, we gather around the altar to thank our ancestors for the rain we've had today.

As I wash before bed, my mother lights a fire on the clay floor. When the fire dies, she sweeps away the ashes and spreads blankets in their place. I burrow into the warm blankets and fall asleep.

3000 BCE
Silk-making begins in China

2800 BCE
Solar eclipses recorded by Chinese astronomers

2697–2597 BCE
The possibly mythical Yellow Emperor Huang Di rules

2000–400 BCE
China's Bronze Age

1700 BCE
The Battle of Mingtiao, in which the Tzu tribe overthrows the Xia dynasty to establish the Shang dynasty, is fought

1500 BCE
The Chinese correctly calculate the number of days it takes for Earth to rotate around the Sun

1250 BCE
Chariot accident involving Emperor Wu Ding's son

1200 BCE
Approximate year of Lady Hao's death

1100 BCE
Chinese begin cultivating soybeans as a crop

1050 BCE
Shang astronomers first predict eclipses

1043 BCE
The Battle of Muye, where the Zhou attack the Shang capital and win, leads to the end of the Shang dynasty

300 BCE
Anesthesia (medicine for putting people to sleep for surgery) is reportedly first used in China

300 BCE
The first major Chinese medical text is written

221 BCE
The Qin dynasty begins, which puts an official end to the practice of "accompanying in death"

1899 CE
A Chinese antiques dealer discovers writing on oracle bones and gives them to an expert to examine

1912
The emperor of China's final dynasty leaves the throne

1936
Archaeologists find a huge burial pit near Anyang containing two entire ancient chariots, along with the skeletons of four horses and three humans with weapons

1976
Lady Hao's tomb is discovered near the modern city of Anyang. It is one of the best-preserved tombs found from Shang dynasty China, with most of its contents still intact.

GLOSSARY

acupuncture method of stopping pain or curing illness by placing needles into a person's skin at particular points on the body

alchemist person who tries to transform base metals into gold or discover a process for extending human life

archaeologist person who studies the bones, tools, and other objects of ancient people to learn about past human life and activities

astrologer person who studies how the positions of the stars and movements of the planets influence the lives and behavior of people

astronomer person who studies the universe and objects in space

barracks building or group of buildings used to house soldiers

class in society, divisions into which people are grouped based on their wealth, social, and cultural status. Rich people are usually at the top, with poor people closer to the bottom.

cowrie shell sea shell with a smooth, glossy dome and a long, narrow opening

diviner person who uses special powers to predict future events

emperor supreme ruler of an empire or territory

game wild animals, birds, or fish hunted for food or sport

hemp tough fiber of the cannabis plant, used for making coarse fabric

martial art sport or skill that began as a form of self-defense or attack

monsoon seasonal, strong winds that create heavy rainstorms in parts of Asia

mummify preserve a body by embalming it and wrapping it in cloth bandages

peasant poor farmer who has a small piece of land for farming, or any uneducated person of low social status

sacrifice killing of an animal or person as a religious offering to a god

virtue behavior showing high moral standards

wicker twigs that are easily bent to make furniture or figurines

Books

Allan. Tony. *Ancient China* (Cultural Atlas for Young People). New York: Chelsea House, 2007.

Anderson, Dale. *Ancient China* (History in Art). Chicago: Raintree, 2005.

Hollihan-Elliot, Sheila. *The Ancient History of China* (China: The Emerging Superpower). Philadelphia: Mason Crest, 2013.

Web sites

www.chinahighlights.com/travelguide/china-history/the-shang-dynasty.htm
Find a short history of the Shang dynasty with helpful links on this web site.

china.mrdonn.org/index.html
This web site includes games, presentations, and fun facts about ancient China for kids and teachers.

www.historyforkids.org/learn/china/history/shang.htm
Learn about art, architecture, and other aspects of Shang dynasty China on this site.

Places to visit

If you're fortunate enough to visit China, travel back in time at the Yinxu Museum complex, near Anyang. It features 600 artifacts from the Shang dynasty, including bronze vessels, jade pieces, oracle bone cellars, chariot pits, a gallery of oracle bones, and Fu Hao's tomb: www.chinahighlights.com/anyang/attraction/yinxu.htm

You can also learn more about Chinese culture and art at the following museums in the United States:

Freer and Sackler Galleries
1050 Independence Avenue, SW
Washington, D.C. 20013
www.asia.si.edu

The Metropolitan Museum of Art
1000 Fifth Avenue (at 82nd Street)
New York, New York 10028
www.metmuseum.org

INDEX